CHOOSING

Activities to Encourage Responsible Decision Making

Written by Corinne Sanders, O.P.

Illustrated by Darcy Tom

Cover by Darcy Tom
Copyright © Good Apple, Inc., 1985
ISBN No. 0-86653-333-8

Good Apple, Inc.
299 Jefferson Rd.
Parsippany, NJ 07054-0480

Description of Kino Learning Center

Kino Learning Center is a private, nonprofit elementary and secondary school founded in Tucson, Arizona, in 1975, by parents seeking an alternative learning environment for children. The school is staffed by 20 teachers and has an enrollment of 200 students between the ages of 3 and 18.

At Kino Learning Center the students, teachers, and parents form a learning community in which people are bound together in mutual aid, responsibility and cooperation. Freedom exists within this interaction as the liberty persons grant to each other out of their faith in and concern for one another. Such freedom is nourished by mutual respect and appreciation; from it, trust grows and individuality flourishes.

Within the prepared learning environment of the school, each child is free to choose from worthwhile options, a sequence of activities unique to his/her needs and experiences, and in which he/she finds success, interest, and pleasure. Each child is free to develop in the way and at the pace appropriate to his/her needs, abilities, and interests. The school places special stress on individual discovery, on firsthand experience, and on creative work.

At Kino Learning Center, adults and children mutually engaged in the learning process are continually in the process of changing and growing, for to learn is to change. And to experience joy in learning is to delight in life itself, for learning and life are one.

Acknowledgements

Thank you to Sister Judy Bisignano for originating many of the ideas contained in this book. Special thanks to Sandy Webb for typing its manuscript and Darcy Tom for bringing its words to life through creative illustrations. Additional thanks for my family for providing a supportive, caring environment for choices to be made freely.

INTRODUCTION

Many critics of modern society point to the loss of a sense of values as a major cause of contemporary problems. While the blame is often placed on the young and teenaged, all age levels seem to have shifted away from an awareness of where they are going. Today's youth are highly criticized for a behavior which reflects a lack of respect for self and others, a general disregard for people and things. There is a drastic need for adult America to assist its youth to deal with the innumerable areas of confusion and conflict in our modern society. The need for the development of a positive self-image and a value system consistent with one's beliefs and behaviors is a vital part of one's existence and survival.

Values can best be developed through questioning one's own feelings and behaviors as well as discussing and responding to the feelings and behaviors of others. Values can also be developed through making decisions in an atmosphere that allows many choices, invites relevant questions, and encourages respect for self and others.

The development of values must be seen as a lifelong process which recognizes changing circumstances rather than a fixed set of unyielding principles. Rather than reacting to a predetermined, fixed moral code, youngsters must be encouraged to develop a self-determined value system which reflects a respect for self, others, and things.

It is the teachers of a school who set the tone and create the atmosphere that is so necessary and appropriate to values education. Their approach to life, their feelings and responses toward themselves and others, and their attitudes toward all living things and the environment have a profound influence upon the attitudes and behavior of their students. It is in this warm, accepting atmosphere that students are invited to develop a tolerance, acceptance, and genuine concern for themselves, others, and living and nonliving things.

Teachers must create innumerable activities and situations which, while developing skills in academic areas, at the same time lead a child toward a basic understanding and development of humaneness. Helping children to become concerned and actively involved in finding solutions to problems in a cooperative manner is an important aspect of values development.

The activities in this book are designed to assist students to improve their relational skills by better knowing and appreciating themselves, as well as people close to them and throughout the world.

The activities in this book are designed to assist students to become more responsible decision makers and to demonstrate an increased awareness of the choices they make.

As the activities in this book are completed, students will have the opportunity to experience the art of choosing. Students will be asked to set daily goals and evaluate them. They will be asked to evaluate choices they are currently making and to determine the reasons behind their choices. Students will be asked to problem solve by stating the problem, listing and evaluating alternatives and determining consequences. Finally, students will be asked to consider choices that affect not only themselves but others around them.

As the activities in this book are completed, students will have repeated opportunities to affirm each other's uniqueness, capability, and cooperation. This need for a positive self-image, a clearly defined values code, and consistent cooperative beliefs and behaviors is vital for today's youth as they begin to hold a more constructive and positive view of themselves and their world. Herein lies the challenge of the present moment and the hope for all that is worthwhile for generations to come.

MY PERSONAL JOURNEY TOWARD RESPONSIBLE DECISION MAKING

Paste a
photo of
yourself in
this space.

_____

NAME

Date Begun: _____

Date Completed: _____

PURPOSE:

The activities throughout this journey are designed to assist you in becoming a responsible decision maker by learning how to choose freely from alternatives after considering the consequences of your choices.

Before You Begin

Before beginning **My Journey Toward Responsible Decision Making**, complete the following statements by putting checks (✔) in the appropriate boxes.

	USUALLY	OFTEN	SOMETIMES	SELDOM	NEVER
1. I set daily goals and try to accomplish them.					
2. I plan activities that help me reach my goals.					
3. I know my personal strengths and weaknesses.					
4. I build on my strengths and try to improve my weaknesses.					
5. I accomplish what I set out to do.					
6. I give myself credit for taking a risk, even if I fall short of my goal.					
7. I plan good times with good friends.					
8. I make choices to improve my health and wellness.					
9. I make choices to improve my physical environment.					
10. I am actively involved in improving the quality of life for myself and others.					

1. Determining Personal Qualities

- Complete the crossword puzzle that contains some of the personal qualities that might be possessed by a person capable of making responsible decisions.

ACROSS

2. Constructive; not negative
3. Truthful
5. Sure of oneself
6. Having knowledge
9. Tuned in

DOWN

1. Having imagination; inventive
2. Able to wait
4. Conscious of; sensitive to
7. Allowing for mistakes
8. Unwavering

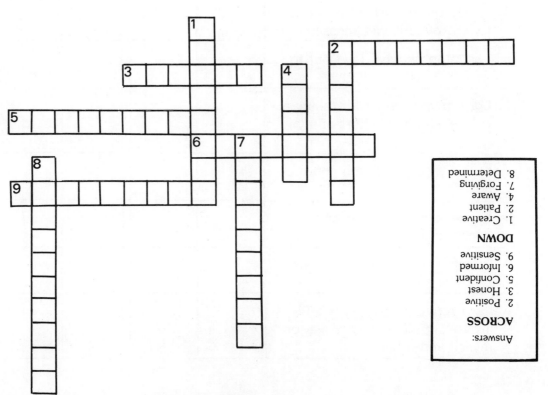

2

2. Describing Myself

- Put an **X** on the line that best describes you.

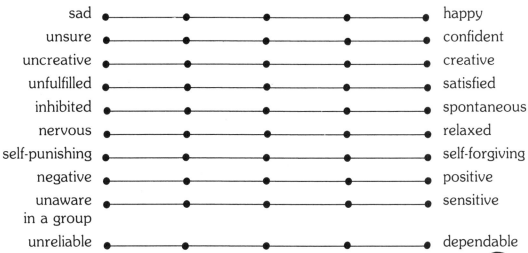

sad				happy
unsure				confident
uncreative				creative
unfulfilled				satisfied
inhibited				spontaneous
nervous				relaxed
self-punishing				self-forgiving
negative				positive
unaware in a group				sensitive
unreliable				dependable

1. kind
2. gentle
3. strong

- Three words that describe me in a positive way are:

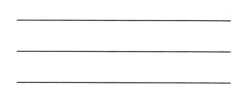

_____

_____

_____

- Three words that describe me in a negative way are:

_____

_____

_____

3. Choosing Feelings

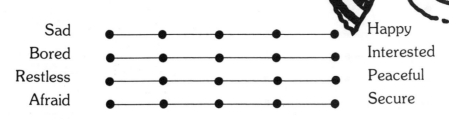

- Put an **X** on the line that indicates your general feelings as a person.

Sad	•——•——•——•——•	Happy
Bored	•——•——•——•——•	Interested
Restless	•——•——•——•——•	Peaceful
Afraid	•——•——•——•——•	Secure

- Complete the sentences that best describe your feelings.

I am most happy when _____

_____

_____

_____

I am most interested in _____

_____

_____

_____

I am most peaceful when _____

_____

_____

_____

I am most secure when _____

_____

_____

_____

4

4. Changing Feelings

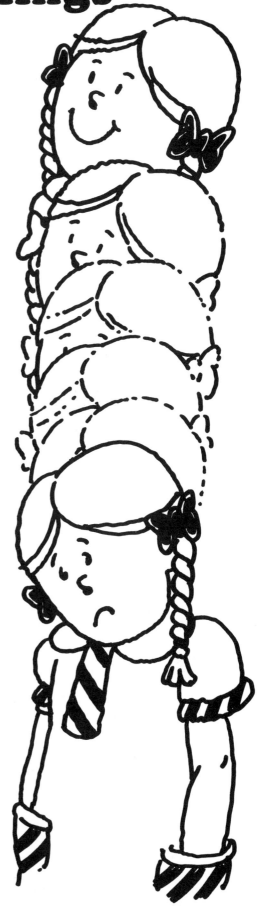

- Tell what you might do to make the following negative feelings more positive.

I am feeling sad and would like to feel more happy.

_____

_____

_____

_____

I am feeling restless and would like to feel more peaceful.

_____

_____

_____

_____

I am feeling afraid and would like to feel more secure.

_____

_____

_____

_____

I am feeling bored and would like to feel more interested.

_____

_____

_____

_____

I am feeling _____ and would like to feel more _____ .

_____

_____

_____

_____

5. Knowing Myself

• Circle the answer that best describes you.

I am generally . . .

a. a likeable person.	YES	NO	UNCERTAIN
b. an informed person.	YES	NO	UNCERTAIN
c. an honest person.	YES	NO	UNCERTAIN
d. a patient person.	YES	NO	UNCERTAIN
e. a forgiving person.	YES	NO	UNCERTAIN
f. a confident person.	YES	NO	UNCERTAIN
g. a determined person.	YES	NO	UNCERTAIN
h. a responsible person.	YES	NO	UNCERTAIN

• Complete the sentence with personal qualities that best describe you.

I am generally . . .

_____

_____

_____

_____

_____

_____

_____

- I believe my greatest strength as a person is:

  _____

  _____

- Three things I could do to build upon this strength are:

  a. _____

  _____

  b. _____

  _____

  c. _____

  _____

- A personal weakness that I could improve upon is:

  _____

  _____

- Three things I could do to improve this weakness are:

  a. _____

  _____

  b. _____

  _____

  c. _____

  _____

My greatest strength is my ability to make people feel happy inside.

6. Taking Control

- Circle the answer that best describes your opinion regarding each statement.

1. Parents should allow their children to make most of their own decisions.   YES   NO   UNCERTAIN

2. If someone doesn't like me I am unable to change that.   YES   NO   UNCERTAIN

3. Planning ahead makes things turn out better.   YES   NO   UNCERTAIN

4. A good way to handle a problem is to ignore it.   YES   NO   UNCERTAIN

5. It's better to be smart than lucky.   YES   NO   UNCERTAIN

6. I can usually count on my horoscope to be correct.   YES   NO   UNCERTAIN

7. I can influence tomorrow by what I do today.   YES   NO   UNCERTAIN

8. Most people are just born good at sports.   YES   NO   UNCERTAIN

9. I have a lot to say about who my friends are.   YES   NO   UNCERTAIN

10. I have little to say about what my family decides.   YES   NO   UNCERTAIN

11. I should be involved in evaluating my school work.   YES   NO   UNCERTAIN

12. Teachers should decide what and when I should learn.   YES   NO   UNCERTAIN

NOTE:

If you answered all the odd numbers with a **yes** and all the even numbers with a **no,** then you are probably in control of your life.

- If you are in control of your life, tell why and how you make this happen.

- If you are **not yet** in control of your life, tell how you might make this happen in the near future.

TAKING CONTROL OF MY LIFE

7. Surveying Wellness

Complete each statement by putting a check (✓) in the box that best describes you.

I eat nutritional meals.

usually ☐
sometimes ☐
seldom ☐
never ☐

I give my body the proper amount and type of exercise.

usually ☐
sometimes ☐
seldom ☐
never ☐

My energy level is usually

high. ☐
moderate. ☐
low. ☐

I am generally

a relaxed person. ☐
a tense person. ☐

Most of the time I cope

very well. ☐
well. ☐
moderately well. ☐
not so well. ☐

I relax my mind and body for at least 20 minutes every day.

usually ☐
sometimes ☐
seldom ☐
never ☐

8. Choosing Wellness

- Based on the Wellness Survey, choose an area of your health that needs improvement.

- Develop your plan to increase wellness in your life.

- Tell about your plan below.

Area of Improvement/Goal: _____

_____

Plan of Action: _____

_____

_____

_____

People and what they can do to help me accomplish my goal:

_____

_____

_____

Date expected to begin plan:

_____

Date expected to accomplish goal:

_____

Expected degree of success in accomplishing my goal:

high ☐

moderate ☐

low ☐

9. Relaxing the Body

When you are tense, situations sometimes appear more complicated than they actually are. As you relax, you are better able to look at a situation and respond with appropriate decision making.

- Complete the following relaxation exercise on a daily basis.

  a. Lie on the floor giving yourself enough space to freely stretch out.

  b. Tense and relax each part of your body. Do this at least three times for each body part: feet, legs, back, neck, hands, and arms.

  c. Continue this procedure until you feel your entire body relaxed for about 20 minutes.

- Tell about your experience below.

10. Relaxing the Mind

- Find a quiet spot out-of-doors.

- Clear your mind of all thoughts by concentrating on the beauty and peacefulness of your physical surroundings.

- Be aware of your senses.

  What do you see?
  What do you hear?
  What do you smell?
  What do you touch?
  What do you taste?

- Choose one sense (hearing, seeing, tasting, smelling, or touching). Use this sense to connect more closely with nature.

- Tell about your experience below.

11. Succeeding

- Tell about something
  important that you
  have accomplished in
  your life.

  _____

  _____

  _____

  _____

  _____

- Why were you successful in accomplishing this goal?

  _____

  _____

  _____

  _____

- If you could repeat this event, what would you do to make it more
  successful than it was originally?

  _____

  _____

  _____

  _____

  _____

  _____

  _____

12. Trying Again!

- Tell about something important that you have tried but failed to accomplish in your life.

_____

_____

_____

_____

- What factors added to your lack of success?

_____

_____

_____

_____

- If you could repeat this event, what would you do to make it more successful than it was originally?

_____

_____

_____

_____

_____

_____

_____

13. Taking a Risk

Complete the following statements by putting checks (✔) in the appropriate boxes.

Before taking a risk . . .	USUALLY	OFTEN	SOMETIMES	SELDOM	NEVER
a. I get all the facts related to the situation.					
b. I think of the possible consequences related to my decision.					
c. I seek the advice of people with more experience related to the situation.					
d. I make sure I am capable of succeeding in the situation.					
e. I consider the necessary safety factors for myself and others.					

- Tell about a time when you took a risk in an irresponsible manner by not considering the factors listed.

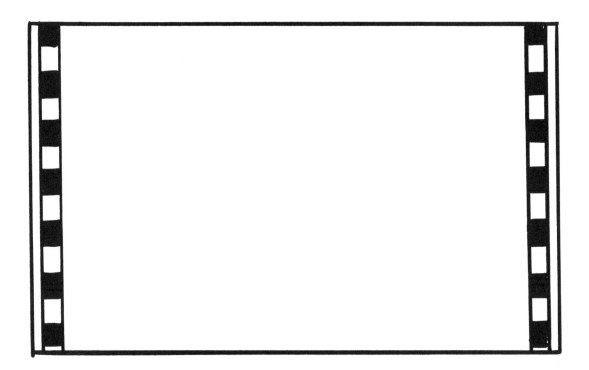

- Tell about a time when you took a risk in a responsible manner by considering the factors listed.

14. Making Choices

Values are the people, things, and activities that are important to me. Responsible choices come from a developed value system.

- Read the statements below.

- Put a **1** next to those statements that are **very important** to you, a **2** next to those statements that are **somewhat important** to you, and a **3** next to those statements that are **not very important** to you.

_____ I like spending time with my family.

_____ I like listening to music.

_____ I like being the leader of a group.

_____ I like being responsible for my decisions.

_____ I like having friends.

_____ I like being alone.

_____ I like taking risks.

_____ I like spending money.

_____ I like learning new things.

_____ I like traveling and seeing new places.

_____ I like helping people.

_____ I like making things.

_____ I like being appreciated.

_____ I like organizing activities.

_____ I like doing things outdoors.

_____ I like working with a group.

_____ I like reading a book.

_____ I like _____

_____ I like _____

15. Determining Values

Name three **people** you care about. Tell why you value these people.

1. _____
   _____
2. _____
   _____
3. _____
   _____

Name three **things** you care about. Tell why you value these things.

1. _____
   _____
2. _____
   _____
3. _____
   _____

Name three **activities** you enjoy. Tell why you value these activities.

1. _____
   _____
2. _____
   _____
3. _____
   _____

16. Making Daily Decisions

- Make a list of all the choices or decisions you make in a single day.

what to eat for breakfast

_____   _____

_____   _____

_____   _____

_____   _____

_____   _____

_____   _____

_____   _____

_____   _____

_____   _____

Put a star (✱) in front of your three most important decisions.

Put a check (✔) in front of your three most enjoyable decisions.

- How many choices do you make in one day? _____
- How many choices do you make in one week? _____
- How many choices do you make in one month? _____
- How many choices do you make in one year? _____

20

17. Setting Daily Goals

Setting daily goals helps me plan my day and use my time wisely.

- Write your goals for one day in the space provided.
- Put an **X** in the box when you accomplish that specific goal.

DAILY GOALS

_____
Date

- ☐ 1 _____
- ☐ 2 _____
- ☐ 3 _____
- ☐ 4 _____
- ☐ 5 _____
- ☐ 6 _____
- ☐ 7 _____
- ☐ 8 _____
- ☐ 9 _____
- ☐ 10 _____

18. Setting Weekly Goals

Setting weekly goals helps me plan my days and use my time wisely.

- Put an **X** in the box when you accomplish each goal.

My Goals for This Week

1 _____

2 _____

3 _____

4 _____

5 _____

6 _____

7 _____

8 _____

9 _____

- Look back through the week. How were you successful?

_____

_____

_____

_____

- How could you have been more successful?

_____

_____

_____

_____

- Did you accomplish a worthy goal? That is, did you do something that contributed to your happiness and welfare or the happiness and welfare of others? Tell about this accomplishment in the space provided.

_____

_____

_____

_____

_____

_____

_____

_____

_____

19. Rewarding Myself

Do you reward yourself when you accomplish your goals and/or solve your problems? _____

- Tell how you might reward yourself for a job well-done in the space provided.

20. Recognizing Support

You are nurtured by the support and recognition other people give you.

- Tell about the support and recognition you have recently received by someone important to you. Who gave you support? Why? What did you do with the support?

- You may want to show this person that you appreciate his/her personal support.

- Tell how you stay encouraged even when others do not recognize your worth and talents. How do you know you are a good person? How do you know when you have been successful in your efforts?

_____

_____

_____

_____

21. Choosing Friends

- List those qualities you desire in a good friend.

- Put a star (✱) in front of the most important quality.

_____   _____

_____   _____

_____   _____

- List those qualities you bring to a friendship.

- Put a star (✱) in front of your most important quality.

22. Resolving Conflict

- Name someone whom you respect and admire.

  _____

- Tell why you admire and respect this person.

  _____

  _____

  _____

Grandma Jacobs

  NOTE: You may want to think of a special way to tell this person how
  important he/she is to you.

- Tell about something you might do to feel rejected by this person.

  _____

  _____

  _____

- Imagine resolving the potential conflict stated above in a positive manner.
  Imagine yourself being successful and accepted, not rejected. Tell about the
  event below.

  _____

  _____

  _____

  _____

  _____

  _____

  _____

  _____

  _____

  _____

23. Choosing Fun

- List 10 activities you enjoy doing in your leisure time.

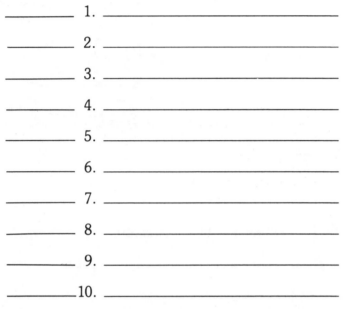

	1.
	2.
	3.
	4.
	5.
	6.
	7.
	8.
	9.
	10.

- Put an **A** before the activities you enjoy doing **a**lone.

- Put a **P** before the activities you enjoy doing with other **p**eople.

- Put a **$** before the activities that cost over $5 each.

- Put an **I** before the activities done **i**ndoors.

- Put an **O** before the activities done **o**utdoors.

- Put a star (✱) before the activity you enjoy the most.

- What general conclusions can you make about your choices for leisure activities?

24. Creating Fun

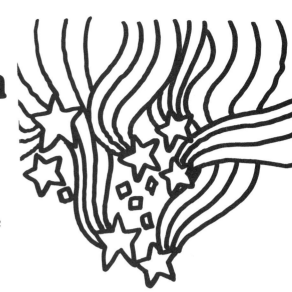

Pretend you have three days to spend any way you like and with anyone you choose. You have enough money to accomplish your goals.

- Write a story about your dream days in the space below.

- Share your story with people whom you care about.

25. Spending Time

- List the number of hours per week that you spend involved in each of the stated activities.

- Put a **1** next to the activity to which you give most of your time; a **2** next to the activity you give the next largest amount of time, etc. Continue this procedure until all activities are numbered.

  NOTE: There are 168 hours in one week.

ACTIVITY	TIME SPENT (hours per week)	TIME PRIORITY
WORKING		
PLAYING		
SLEEPING		
EATING		
OTHER (general activities not considered to be work or play)		

- Draw conclusions about the importance of these activities in your life according to the time you give to each activity.

_____

_____

_____

_____

_____

26. Enjoying Life

Listed below are general recreational activities.

- Rank the three most important activities by putting a star (✱) next to each activity.

- Indicate the time (in hours per week) that you spend on each activity.

- Indicate if the activity is a growing experience by circling YES or NO after each activity.

ACTIVITY	RANK 1-2-3	TIME SPENT	GROWING EXPERIENCE
reading for pleasure			YES NO
talking with friends			YES NO
watching television			YES NO
attending parties			YES NO
being alone			YES NO
_____			YES NO
_____			YES NO
_____			YES NO
_____			YES NO
_____			YES NO

27. Worrying About Life

It is normal to be concerned about the uncertain aspects of your life.

- Identify your areas of worry by marking one box for each item listed.

I WORRY ABOUT	OFTEN	SOMETIMES	NEVER
my general appearance.			
my parents growing old.			
some past things I have done.			
being attacked and/or robbed.			
losing my good friends.			
getting sick.			
what people think about me.			
something happening to my family.			
snakes and spiders, etc.			
dying.			
having the money I need.			
failing at what I try.			
nuclear war.			
my parent(s) keeping a job.			
going to college.			

- Name three of your biggest worries in the space below.

_____

_____

_____

28. Solving Small Problems

- Tell about one small nagging thing that you often worry about.

  _____

  _____

  _____

- What is the **worst** that could happen as a result of this situation?

  _____

  _____

  _____

  _____

- What is the **best** that could happen as a result of this situation?

  _____

  _____

  _____

  _____

- What can you do to make the best, rather than the worst, thing happen?

  _____

  _____

  _____

  _____

- Put your plan into action. Work at and expect to solve this nagging problem in your life.

29. Solving Large Problems

- List one situation that causes you a great deal of concern and worry.

  _____

  _____

  _____

  _____

- Is it possible for you to improve this situation?

  Yes _____ No _____ Uncertain _____

- Try breaking the large problem into many smaller parts. Next, write what action you will take to solve each smaller aspect of the larger problem.

  _____

  _____

  _____

  _____

  _____

  _____

  _____

  _____

  _____

  _____

- Put your plan into action. Work at and expect to solve, or greatly improve, your problem.

30. Lessening Worries

- Is it possible for you to worry less about the problems in your life?

  Yes _____ No _____ Uncertain _____

- If possible, devise a plan to improve how you react to the worry in your life. Tell about the kinds of relaxation that work best for you.

  _____

  _____

  _____

  _____

  _____

  _____

  _____

  _____

  _____

  _____

  _____

- How do you feel now that you are planning and improving your situation rather than worrying about it? Do you have more energy? Do you feel more productive? Are you more successful?

  _____

  _____

  _____

  _____

35

31. Stating Goals, Problems and Solutions

"wanna play, sis?"

Taking charge of your life requires that you set goals, identify obstacles to reaching these goals, and determine solutions to these obstacles. State your goals, your problem, your solution to both of the situations described.

Scenario #1 — You have a younger sister or brother who always wants to play with you. You are 3 years older than s/he and enjoy activities with your own friends.

My goal: _____

My problem: _____

_____

_____

My solution: _____

_____

_____

Scenario #2 — For years you have wanted to play on your school's basketball team. Finally you are chosen for the team, but practices are at the same time as play practice. You enjoy acting and your teacher has offered you the lead in this year's play.

My goal: _____

My problem: _____

_____

_____

My solution: _____

_____

_____

32. My Goal, Problem and Solution

GOAL

- Take greater charge of your life by setting a goal, identifying obstacles to reaching this goal, and determining a solution to these obstacles. State your situation below.

My goal: _____

_____

_____

_____

My problem: _____

_____

_____

_____

_____

_____

_____

_____

My solution: _____

_____

_____

_____

_____

_____

- Ask your teacher and classmates to help you further clarify your goal-setting and problem-solving techniques.

33. Determining Alternatives

There are usually several ways to achieve your goals.

- List three ways to accomplish each goal stated below.

- List an advantage and disadvantage for each suggestion.

Goal #1: To acquire clothes

SUGGESTIONS FOR GOAL	ADVANTAGES OF SUGGESTIONS	DISADVANTAGES OF SUGGESTIONS

Goal #2: To enjoy the weekend

SUGGESTIONS FOR GOAL	ADVANTAGES OF SUGGESTIONS	DISADVANTAGES OF SUGGESTIONS

34. Making Decisions

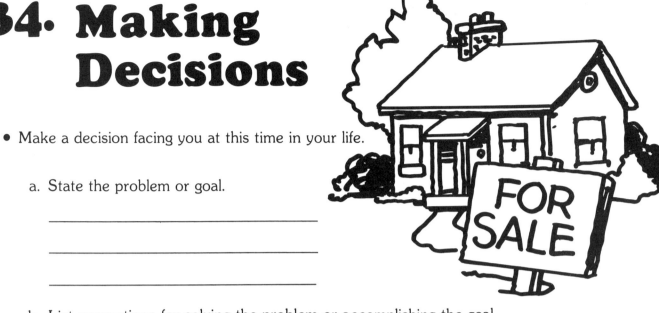

• Make a decision facing you at this time in your life.

   a. State the problem or goal.

   _____

   _____

   _____

   b. List suggestions for solving the problem or accomplishing the goal.

   State the advantages and disadvantages of each suggestion.

SUGGESTIONS	ADVANTAGES OF SUGGESTIONS	DISADVANTAGES OF SUGGESTIONS

   c. Choose one solution for solving your problem or one suggestion for meeting your goal.

   I choose to _____

   _____

   _____

35. Making Consumer Choices

• A consumer item is a product that you buy and use. Using words and pictures from magazines and newspapers, create a collage of the various examples of a single consumer product. You may want to show the many choices of toothpaste or the variety of breakfast cereals.

36. Being an Informed Consumer

- Investigate the specific brands of the product chosen for your collage in the previous activity. Consider such factors as eye appeal, color, taste (if applicable), ingredients, cost, etc. Record your observations below.

Consumer Product: _____

BRAND NAME	POSITIVE FACTORS	NEGATIVE FACTORS

- After investigating various brands of a specific product, which brand would you choose if you were to buy this product?

_____

_____

37. Choosing the Good Life

What is the good life? What would you own? What would you do?
Where would   you live? What kind of person would you be?

- List several activities of the good life for you.

_____
_____
_____
_____
_____
_____
_____
_____
_____
_____
_____
_____
_____

- Put a check (✔) before those activities
  you presently do on a regular basis.
- Put a star (✱) before the activity you value
  most.
- Discuss with your teachers and classmates
  what the good life means to you and them.
- Discuss if and how it might be possible to
  live the good life with little or no material
  wealth.

38. Creating the Good Life

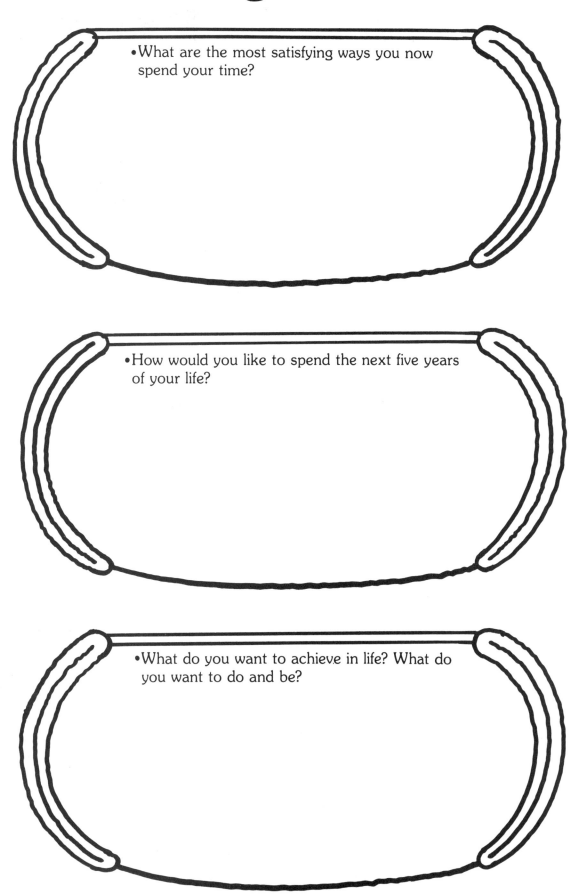

• What are the most satisfying ways you now spend your time?

• How would you like to spend the next five years of your life?

• What do you want to achieve in life? What do you want to do and be?

39. Stating Life Goals

- State three important life goals in their order of importance.

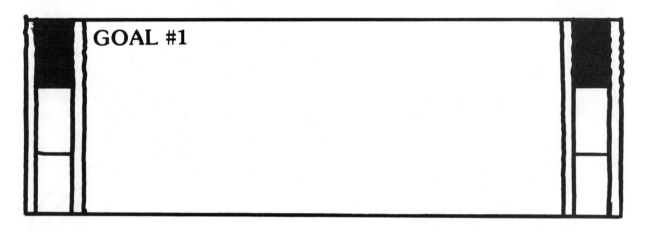

GOAL #1

GOAL #2

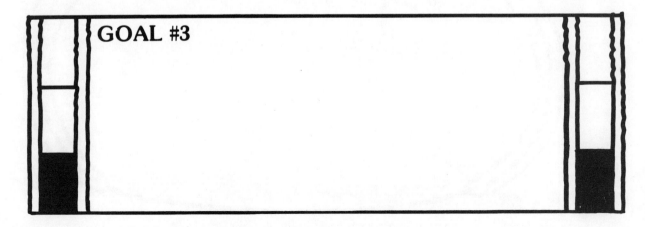

GOAL #3

40. Making It Happen

- State one of your three life goals in the space below:

  GOAL: _____

  _____

- List those activities that will assist you in accomplishing this goal.

  _____

  _____

  _____

  _____

  _____

  _____

  _____

- List those obstacles that might prevent you from fully accomplishing your goal.

  _____

  _____

  _____

  _____

  _____

- List the support, training, skills, etc., that will help you accomplish your goal.

  _____

  _____

  _____

  _____

  _____

41. Improving My Environment

- Tell how your physical environment promotes your health, happiness, and personal growth.

_____

_____

_____

_____

_____

- Tell how your physical environment hinders your health, happiness, and personal growth.

_____

_____

_____

_____

_____

- Choose one thing you can do to improve or beautify your physical environment. State your goal below.

_____

_____

_____

- Devise a plan to make your goal a reality. Tell about your plan in the space provided.

_____

_____

_____

_____

_____

_____

- Document the improvement you have made to your physical environment. You may want to take "before" and "after" photographs showing the problem and your solution or improvement of the problem.

42. Becoming Aware

The daily newspapers are filled with issues and problems on a local, state, national, and global level that affect you personally.

- Read the newspapers and reports on a local issue or problem. State the problem below.

- Record the circumstances related to the problem as well as the decision made to solve the problem.

- Do you agree or disagree with the solution to the problem? Record your response below.

LOCAL ISSUE

The Problem: _____

_____

The Circumstances: _____

_____

_____

_____

The Solution: _____

_____

My Response: _____

_____

_____

• Repeat this procedure for a state or national issue and a global issue.

STATE OR NATIONAL ISSUE

The Problem: _____
_____

The Circumstances: _____
_____
_____

The Solution: _____
_____

My Response: _____
_____

WORLD ISSUE

The Problem: _____
_____

The Circumstances: _____
_____
_____

The Solution: _____
_____

My Response: _____
_____

43. Becoming Involved

Once you become aware of important issues, you may choose to **become involved** in their solutions. For example, children often participate in local and national efforts to raise money to cure illness and alleviate world hunger.

- Find a newspaper article about children becoming involved in local, national, or global issues. Tell about the event in the space provided.

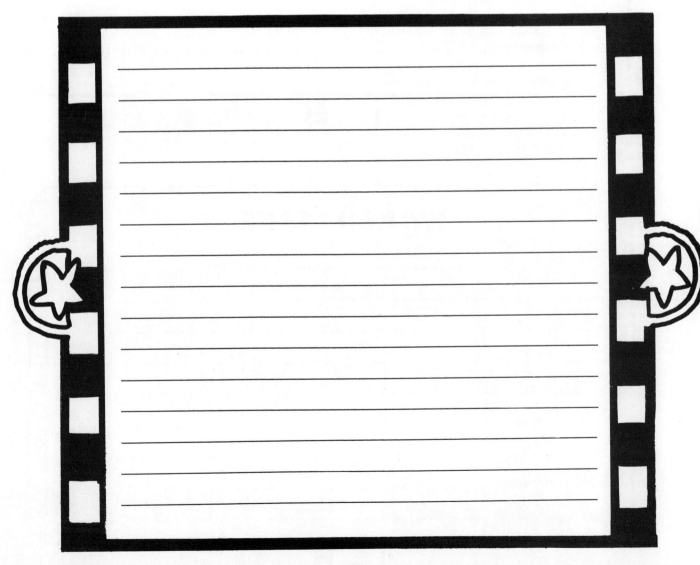

- You may want to join with other children to improve the quality of life for yourself and others on a local, national, or global level.

- Tell about your project to bring about human good in the space below.

44. Choosing Change

Put a check(✔) in the appropriate box.

I desire to improve . . .	STRONGLY	SOMEWHAT	NOT AT ALL
the way I feel about myself.			
the way I relate to friends.			
the way I relate to my family.			
my learning at school.			
my personal appearance.			
my physical health.			
the way I resolve conflict.			
the way I solve problems.			
_____			
_____			
_____			
_____			

45. Creating Your Future

CHANGE HELPS US GROW!

- Choose an area from activity 44 in which you desire to create change. In the space below, formulate a plan of action to make this change occur.

My goal for change: _____

_____

   a. I desire this change because: _____

      _____

   b. The benefits of this change would be: _____

      _____

      _____

- List one person who could help you reach your goal.

- Tell how this person could help you reach your goal.

   Name: _____

   _____

   _____

- Write your plan of action for creating your future.

_____

_____

_____

_____

_____

- You may want to put your plan into action. Your future is now.

46. Planning Ahead

The time line indicates 100 years marked at 5- year intervals.

- Tell about the interesting and important events of your past.

Year I was born

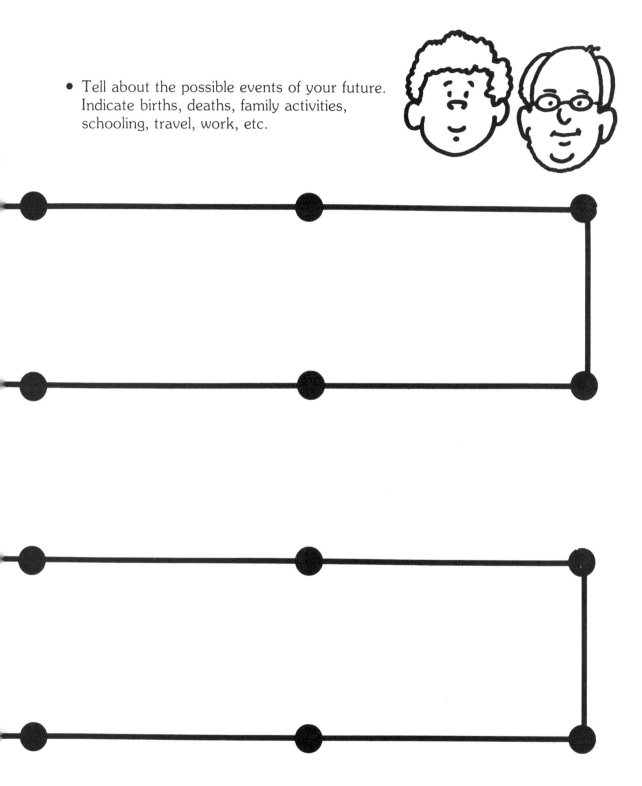

- Tell about the possible events of your future. Indicate births, deaths, family activities, schooling, travel, work, etc.

Final Summary

- State three things you have learned about yourself as a result of completing **My Personal Journey Toward Responsible Decision Making.**

1. _____

   _____

2. _____

   _____

3. _____

   _____

After completing this book, my **desire** to become a responsible decision maker is

- ☐ More.

- ☐ Less.

- ☐ About the same.

After completing this book my **ability** to become a responsible decision maker is

- ☐ More.

- ☐ Less.

- ☐ About the same.

After finishing **My Journey Toward Responsible Decision Making,** complete the following statements by putting a check (✓) in the appropriate box.

	USUALLY	OFTEN	SOMETIMES	SELDOM	NEVER
1. I set daily goals and try to accomplish them.					
2. I plan activities that will help me reach my goals.					
3. I know my personal strengths and weaknesses.					
4. I build on my strengths and try to improve my weaknesses.					
5. I accomplish what I set out to do.					
6. I give myself credit for taking a risk, even if I fall short of my goal.					
7. I plan fun times with special friends.					
8. I make choices to improve my health and wellness.					
9. I make choices to improve my physical environment.					
10. I am actively involved in improving the quality of life for myself and others.					

By No Means the End

Although we consistently make choices to grow toward responsible decision making, we never really complete our journey toward this end.

- Tell how you intend to continue your journey toward responsible decision making.